S0-BCO-411

WHY OWN A CHIHUAHUA?

Why own a Chihuahua? Why indeed! There are all sorts of reasons as to why people choose Chihuahuas. In my own instance I wanted a Great Dane, so my husband promptly gave me a Chihuahua! A gift I never regretted. Most people do not really know what breed they want, nor why. It is usually force of circumstances. Perhaps you've seen a charming Chihuahua, and, given the time, the opportunity and the inclination, you decide that this dog is the one for you. And once a dog is yours it is the only breed on earth that is perfect.

Most people have no idea how to pronounce "Chihuahua," and curious pronunciations are applied to it from time to time:

The tiny Chihuahua is the smallest breed of dog in the world. Its vast legion of owners will also argue that it is the most charming of all breeds.

Chee-hooa-hooas, Chincilla, Chee, Chigh, and so on. The correct pronunciation, however, used in Mexico, the land of their origin, is "Chee-*waa*-wa."

Of all the breeds in the world, the Chihuahua is the smallest. There is none other so compact, so charming or so intelligent. He is like quicksilver in his observations and his energy, and there is nothing that he loves more than to be constantly loved, and to be with his owner.

There are two varieties of Chihuahua, the Long Coat and the Smooth Coat. The Smooth Coat was the original Mexican Chihuahua and is more popular in the United States, but the Long Coat is proving more popular in Great Britain. As far as general care and grooming

The Chihuahua's coat can come in just about any color. The type of coat can be either Long Coat, as shown above, or Smooth Coat.

A Chihuahua absolutely radiates personality, and he will give so much and expect so little in return. His alertness and devotion are unbounding, and he is by no means a yappy, snappy, spoiled little toy dog unless his owner makes him so. Nor is he quarrelsome; he will get on well with other animals such as parakeets, cats, rabbits, and other dogs of all sizes, always provided that his owner will allow him to.

Chihuahuas are not roamers, and they love their comfort perhaps more than all other dogs. They hate to be left alone for long, and they love a cozy, comfortable bed, particularly one with a soft blanket in which to bury themselves. They are not scratchers nor are they destructive in any way. They are concerned, a Chihuahua could hardly be easier to manage.

The Chihuahua makes an excellent watchdog, since he has a keen sense of hearing and excellent sight. His olfactory senses, on the other hand, are by no means acute. In fact, his sense of smell can be so bad that a tasty bone placed three inches out of range may take him a few seconds to find.

Chihuahuas are extraordinarily hardy little dogs, not susceptible to any particular illnesses other than the normal canine ones. They are remarkably long-lived, often reaching 14 to 19 years of age.

This is an example of the Smooth Coat variety. Regardless of coat type or color, the Chihuahua is an extraordinarily hardy dog with a radiant personality.

love warmth and can travel in an enclosed box that other dogs would not tolerate, and they are perfectly happy to be secreted into places where dogs are "not

the O.K. that all is well, and that they can reveal themselves.

Chihuahuas can anticipate moods perhaps better than any other dog because they are so

Chihuahuas are happy to share their home with each other or other pets. They will be quite content as long as they have a soft, cozy bed to bury themselves in.

allowed," hidden carefully beneath the fold of a scarf, or under a coat. It is quite extraordinary how they know when they must be silent; they will keep as quiet as a mouse, never moving a whisker until their owners have given them

sensitive; a harsh tone of voice can bring them untold misery. Loving, tiny and adoring as he may be, surprisingly a Chihuahua is really a sporting dog; he will challenge breeds like the Great Dane and think that he can do so with impunity; or he will go with the men of the family on an 18-hole round of golf, loving every moment of the game. He also has the facility of being quite happy and content as a cuddly lap dog sitting amidst platinum, mink and satins, if this is what his owner prefers. But he is not really a snob at heart, and if mink and emeralds and diamonds are missing, he is such a charming little dog that he will adore his penniless owner if only he is adored in return.

A Chihuahua always attracts attention from dog lovers, and passers-by frequently stop to admire him. If he is a well-bred specimen, his proud owner will find himself discussing animatedly

The Chihuahua is extremely eager to make new acquaintances. Its engaging personality attracts all types of people—even a very shy person cannot turn away from the Chihuahua's fervent friendliness.

his dog's illustrious pedigree with anyone interested. To the shy and to the introvert, a Chihuahua will bring quick contact with other people, especially if there is a common bond; newly made friends are quickly ensnared.

It is fun to study the dog's personality and winning ways. It is particularly interesting to observe him and to watch the way he thinks, and the way he will ask for things, which he will do beautifully with his eyes and sometimes with his voice, which is not quite so beautiful! Perceptive observation will give the owner so much pleasure, if he notices, for example, the way that the Chihuahua carries his tail, or how he wags it from side to side, fast or slow, the whole of it, or just the tip. Each movement indicates some emotion, whether it be sad, happy, frightened, miserable, pathetic or joyous. If his ears are observed carefully they will reveal his feelings in a miraculous way, both in health and when he is ill, or when he is aggressive, pleased or shy. Pleasure and great understanding between owner and dog can be achieved by observation of a Chihuahua's moods, and there are no two

The diminutive size of the Chihuahua makes it an ideal pet for apartments, small homes, and tiny yards.

Chihuahuas with identical characteristics. They can "talk" perhaps with more ease than any other breed, if their owner is only willing to listen.

If their master is going on vacation, it is usually easy to find a friend who will care for them; or better still, the Chihuahuas can go along, while larger breeds may have to be put into boarding kennels.

Owing to their diminutive size, Chihuahuas are excellent for small homes and tiny yards, and they are extremely easy to cope with in apartments. Like all dogs they love to walk and to rush around restricted by a leash. They are extremely accommodating, perfectly willing to walk their owner off his feet with a three- or four-mile walk, or quite content to take things very gently, or merely to race around a room, a balcony or a small garden. Chihuahuas do not, however, appreciate being kept

Because Chihuahuas are not roamers and would rather snuggle than scurry about, they are ideal lap dogs who love to cuddle with their masters.

for long in a pen. They obviously remember their early carefree Mexican past when their ancestors basked lazily in the sun underneath their favorite cactus. They are game to chase the cat; often they have more courage than common sense, when they like to run off a dog of some large breed, particularly a long-coated one. This enchanting dog has made his way into the hearts of many famous people, from His Imperial Highness Haile Selassie of Ethiopia to Xavier Cugat and the late Jayne Mansfield.

The only home where a Chihuahua perhaps is not advisable except with special precautions is one in which there are very young children. This applies to all small breeds, unless the children are carefully supervised so that they cannot inadvertently harm the animal. This can happen all too easily, and if a small child picks up a wriggling puppy and accidentally drops it, or a husky little boy should perhaps accidentally kick a Chihuahua, immeasurable damage can result. Until the children are prepared to undertake the handling and loving care which must be extended toward a Chihuahua puppy, it is best to delay its purchase. But once a child understands that gentle handling is needed, they soon become inseparable companions. Chihuahuas are excellent dogs for the elderly, especially for those suffering from rheumatism or arthritis, as they are light to pick up and easy to manage.

The Chihuahua is small and easily injured, so it is important that very young children be carefully supervised and taught the proper way of handling their pint-sized pet.

Some dog lovers suffering from certain types of asthma believe that they are allergic to all dogs and do not dare keep one, only to discover that the Chihuahua, of all breeds, does not enhance their suffering and that it can be kept safely as a pet.

Cultured people through the centuries, particularly women, have always kept, loved and been adored by toy dogs. This is still true in this modern time of rush, hurry and bustle, when cultured and discerning people have fallen for this endearing little dog whose character and boldness surpass his tiny frame.

It is strange how often one hears people grandly announce that they like only large dogs, then quickly modify their opinion when owned by a Chihuahua. This includes people who have kept all kinds of breeds, big and little; when they fall for a Chihuahua it is forever, because it is undoubtedly the sweetest and most charming breed of all and knows it. If you are not owned by a Chihuahua, change your way of life right now.

ORIGIN OF THE CHIHUAHUA

Only in comparatively recent times was the Chihuahua given its present name, so it is not too easy to trace its history. There is little doubt, however, that the Smooth Coat Chihuahua is of Mexican origin, although there are theories that it originated in Europe. These are based on the erroneous assumption that there were no dogs in Mexico at the time of the Spanish Conquest. There were, in fact, many dogs there at that time.

Like most breeds of dog, the Smooth Coat Chihuahua has changed considerably over the centuries, but it has for the most part retained two out of its three original distinctive features. These are the molera in the skull (that is, an open fontanel), the flat furry tail that exists in no other breed, and the curious foot with extra-long metacarpals and long curving nails. This unusual foot has, unfortunately, not been retained;

It is assumed that the Smooth Coat Chihuahua evolved in Mexico somewhere around the time of the Spanish Conquest.

however, the modern, smaller Chihuahua foot does look neater.

The molera, although curious, is of no advantage, but it is still to be found in most Chihuahuas, although less frequently in the Long Coat variety. Generally speaking, the smaller the Chihuahua, the larger the molera and, occasionally, there are several moleras in the skull.

The flat furry tail, often an inch to an inch and a half wide at the center and furriest part, is also still to be found in most Chihuahuas. Since it is an idiosyncracy of the breed, it would be a great pity if it were ever allowed to disappear.

The Smooth Coat Chihuahua has been developed to its present standard by American breeders during this century. In the early days, the tiny Smooth Coat was exceedingly rare. Often they were not physically sound. Consequently, American breeders had to incorporate other breeds in order to produce stronger and sounder stock, particularly for showing purposes.

Up until 1935, there was an undoubtedly strong terrier influence in the breed; this can still be seen occasionally in lobes, and the round, rat-like tail; and its influence was once seen in the longer length of leg. However, owing to interbreeding in the early part of this century, Smooth Coat Chihuahuas have gradually become sounder and truer to type, and there has been

Evidence of a strong terrier influence in the Chihuahua's evolution is apparent by large ear lobes, round rat-like tails, and the black and tan coloring that some Chihuahuas have in their coats.

Chihuahuas with typical terrier markings and movement. The English Black and Tan Toy Terrier was another breed which influenced the Chihuahua. This can still be noted in the black and tan coloring, especially in the tan spots on the cheek, the large ear no need for many years to incorporate other breeds.

The Long Coat Chihuahua is entirely an American-made breed, and how very beautiful and charming it is too. Since there were only smooth-coated Chihuahuas in Mexico, it was

The Long Coat Chihuahua owes its flowing long coat to crosses that were purposely done in the early 1900s with the Papillon (shown above). Many Long Coat Chihuahuas today still resemble the Papillon in color, markings, and facial features.

Apart from these main outcrosses, there may have been crosses a long time ago with the Pekingese, the Yorkshire Terrier and even, surprisingly, with the Poodle. These, however, seem to have had very little influence on the breed. There is no doubt, however, that the Long Coat Chihuahua is now a most attractive little dog, particularly when it retains the outstanding features of the true Chihuahua and does not resemble any other toy breed.

EARLY HISTORY

There were certainly dogs in Mexico and Central America thousands of years before the Spanish Conquest. Dogs of all sizes and colors, and particularly the hairless variety, were used by many Indians in their festivals, feasts and religious ceremonies. The Xoloitzcuintli is still found there in three sizes, the largest ones being the normal size of approximately 24 inches at the shoulder, the Miniature stands 13 to 18 inches, and the smallest one, called the Mexican Hairless, stands 11 to 12 inches. These dogs are often confused with the tiny Chihuahua, and in some cases, people have thought that Chihuahuas and the Mexican Hairless dogs were the same, but this is not so. The hairless dogs probably reached Mexico by two or three different ways at different times. The first people to reach Mexico and Central America, of whom there is any knowledge, were migrants from Asia who crossed the Bering Strait from

obvious that, in order to produce a long-coated Chihuahua, crosses with long-coated breeds were necessary. In the early days of this century the chief breeds used for this evolution were the Papillon and the Pomeranian. Until a few years ago, many Long Coat Chihuahuas much resembled the Papillon in color, marking, the more closely set eyes, the longer snipy muzzle, and the long straggly ear-fringes. The Pomeranian influence can be seen in the color of the wolf sables, in the small eyes, and in the gait and proportion of the hind legs.

The Pomeranian (above) was crossed with the Chihuahua in the beginning of the 20th century to produce the Long Coat variety. Evidence of this crossing can be seen in the color of wolf sable Chihuahuas, small eyes, gait and proportion of the hind legs.

Siberia to Alaska about 25,000 BC. These people came over in several waves and were big-game hunters, and they may well have brought some of their dogs with them. It took 600 generations and 18,000 years before some of the migrants eventually reached the tip of South America, a distance of 11,000 miles, in about 7000 BC.

Another way that the hairless dogs may have reached Mexico is with the seafaring people of the Chin dynasty of China, who flourished about 400 BC, and they too could have brought hairless dogs with them. Hairless dogs may also have reached there in the 18th century when Chinese merchants settled on the west coast of Mexico; they could have introduced their Chinese Crested dogs then too. It is interesting that the hairless dogs found in this area are known as China Peloña, meaning Chinese Hairless dog. But this may possibly have been the name that the Chinese gave these dogs which were similar to their own variety; the name China Peloña is often heard in Mexico to this day.

The first important people who lived in Mexico were the Mayas around 4000 BC. Later they lived

Below is an example of the Xoloitzcuintli (or Mexican Hairless), a hairless dog of Mexican origin whose genesis is likely tied into the tiny Chihuahua.

These are two pre-Cortesian statuettes, called "dogs" by some archaeologists. A number of similar statuettes belonging to ancient cultures seem to prove the existence of man's best friend in primitive societies of yesterday.

in Guatemala and Honduras and flourished in Yucatan about 600 AD. The rise and fall of the second Mayan culture was from 900 to 1450 AD. Some of the Mayan references to dogs are particularly interesting. The Mayan god of death, Ah Puch, who was similar to the Aztec god of death, Mictlantecutli, presided over the nine underworlds, and his constant companions were a dog, a moan bird and an owl. All these creatures were of evil omen to the Mayas. If the Mayan Muluc years were bad, they held a ceremony in which the old women performed a dance on stilts, and then the gods were offered pottery dogs with food placed on their backs. The cocoa plantation owners also held a sacrifice to the cocoa god. Chocolate-spotted dogs were used if possible, and the

poor dog was hurled from the top of a pyramid into a pile of stones below. The heart was immediately cut out and placed between two plates, and then offered as a sacrifice to the cocoa god. The dog was also used on the Mayan calendar, but the day of the dog was not considered a happy one. "Don't marry a man born on the day Oc (the day of the dog) for he will stray from home often."

At the time of the Spanish Conquest, the Mayan dogs in Yucatan seem to have consisted of two types of Greyhound, described as mostly red in color. The small ones were used as watchdogs and the large ones for hunting. The Mayas also had hairless dogs which were called Xulos, and these were bred in certain districts and kept in herds like cattle. The females were kept for breeding, but most of the males were castrated and fattened for marketing.

The first books to be produced in Middle America were hieroglyphic writings, and they are known as codices and lienzos. The earliest Mayan ones were compiled about 1000 AD. Unfortunately, there are only three Mayan codices in existence, compared to 50 Aztec, Zapotec and Mixtec codices. The Mayan books of Chilam Balem, the book from the Guatemalan Quiché Indians, Popol Vuh, and the divine book of the Toltecs, Teoamoxtli, are unfortunately the only ones which were left. The Spanish Conquistadors in the 16th century and, later, the priests, destroyed a tremendous number of the old Indian codices. The Mayas did not draw exactly what they saw; they blended the features of humans, animals and plants into a type of caricature, so that all dogs looked alike, and all crocodiles, parrots, etc., were

Though the Smooth Coat Chihuahua's ancestry dates back several hundred years, the Long Coat is a relatively recent development in the United States.

symbolic, so that it is difficult for anyone to know precisely the type of dog they were depicting.

The next great culture was that of the Toltecs. This is a modern name given to a group of people who lived about 700 BC in the area of Tula, which was their capital until it was eventually destroyed by fire and abandoned in 1150 AD.

During the 12th century there was a great southward movement in North America. Some of the tribes, which were much later given the name of the Chichimecs (sons of the dogs) because they were barbarians and knew nothing of agriculture and weaving, finally settled in the area of the Toltecs. These people had a mythological god Kukulcan or Quetzalcoatl, as he was also called. He seems to have been fair-haired and lived in Tula where he built his palaces of silver and shells. He eventually departed from the land, burying his treasure there and promising the people that he would one day return to them. This legend was handed down through generations, and when the Spaniards arrived, many of the Indians believed it was Quetzalcoatl returning to them. This is one of the reasons why a handful of Spaniards were able to conquer Mexico so easily.

THE AZTECS

All the Chichimecs spoke the Nahuatl language, of which there were 35 dialects. Amongst these people was a poor Indian tribe known as the Aztecs or Mexicas. The tribe had been wandering for over 200 years and was passing through the area of the Valley of Mexico in 1325. Weary of its wandering, the tribe eventually arrived at the marshy western shore of a swamp, Tlalcocomoco on Lake Tezcoco. Here they found a stone where, 40 years earlier, a priest had sacrificed Prince Copil. From this stone had sprung a Nopal cactus. One of the advance guards of the Aztecs saw an eagle sitting on this Nopal cactus holding in his beak a serpent: this was the long awaited sign which had been prophesied. It was to be

A statuette purporting to be an Itzcuintli, or Aztec dog. Courtesy of Museo Nacional, Mexico City.

the place where they were to settle and to build their city. One of the priests, impelled by some divine power, dived into the pool and held an interview with Tlaloc, god of the rain and waters, who gave them permission to settle there. It was here that the Aztecs built their capital, Tenochtitlan, and began their mighty empire, which flourished from 1428 until it was conquered by the Spaniards in 1521.

The religions throughout the middle Americas were very similar. As in all primitive religions, the elements and the sun and the moon were worshipped. All seem to have used the dog in one way or other, different breeds being used by different tribes. The Aztecs believed that the sun, called Ipainomohuani, was the source of all life and was in constant nightly battle with the stars, and that it therefore needed to be recharged with life every day. So, the Aztecs presented the sun with humans and animals, and later with just their bleeding hearts. At the height of the Aztec power, their human victims seem to have averaged 200 a day.

At the time of the Spanish Conquest the population of middle America was between 12 and 15 million Indians, and the Aztec territory covered 130,000 square miles. Between 1519 and 1634, however, two-thirds of the Indian population perished, mostly from European diseases. After the Conquest there were a number of chroniclers, but most of them were barely literate and often ignorant and bigoted fools; few of them have been accurate in their writings. It was difficult for them to contend with 250 languages and many animals which they had never seen before. It is, therefore, extremely difficult trying to sort fact from fiction. In addition, many of the authors copied from one another for two or three hundred years.

Some of the Indians used small hairless dogs and pottery effigies for their burials, and many of these are found in the Mexican State of Colima. This is three mountain ranges and hundreds of miles from the Aztec territory. These ancient burial places were called Xoloteupan. Over 500 clay pottery dogs have been found there, and there are probably thousands more in the area. Most of these dogs are small, round and hairless. They seem to have been buried with the Indians in place of a real dog. Carbon 14 tests have proved that the figurines are from 500 to 3,000 years old. They seem to depict the fattened, castrated hairless dogs, although some of them show a full set of teeth which, of course, the hairless dog does not have. Many of these clay dogs are roach-backed. They were often molded as water jars with the mouth, the tail or an opening in the head as the spout. One of these pottery figures depicts a little hairless dog fighting a little hairy one, so perhaps this little hairy one was a Chihuahua. It seems unlikely as the shape of the skull is so different, but then dogs change over the centuries.

One of the oldest figures of a Chihuahua dog is to be seen in the National Museum in Mexico. It is a 3,000-year-old figure of a tiny dog kissing his master on the mouth, and it was found at Tlatico. Perhaps the most

This clay pottery dog is said to antedate Columbus. Its size and shape suggest that its subject might have been an ancestor of the Chihuahua.

charming model of all is the one of a Mayan woman walking along holding her little child by the hand, while tucked under her other arm is a tiny prick-eared dog. This was found in Chiapas and dates back to 750 AD.

Skeletons of dogs of all sizes have been found in graves in many parts of Mexico and Central America. There is a very good drawing of the excavation at Kaminaljuyu just outside Guatemala City. This shows the skeletons of a man, three children, and a dog who were found together with the usual funeral paraphernalia for the next world.

Contrary to some of the writings on the dogs of Mexico, there is no doubt at all that there were many dogs in Mexico at the time of the Aztecs, and there seems no reason to believe that the little yellow sacred dog was other than the original Chihuahua. Some writers have tried to prove that Chihuahuas originated in Europe and were brought over to Mexico by the Spaniards. Undoubtedly, the Spaniards brought dogs to Mexico, the first of these being a

Although Mexicans insist that the Chihuahua is in no way a European breed, the English Toy Spaniel (shown) seems to share lineage with the Chihuahua. It is possible that Spaniards brought Chihuahuas back to Europe and somehow these two breeds were crossed.

Greyhound. They also took battle dogs. But since there is such good evidence that the Aztecs used little yellow dogs as sacrifices for their funerals, it seems pointless to try to prove that the Chihuahua originated in Europe. Mexicans are firm in their belief that the Chihuahua is in no way a European dog. It is far more likely that the Smooth Coat Chihuahua was taken back to Europe by the Spaniards since some are still found on the islands of Malta, Sardinia and in Venice. Some of the original Smooth Coat Chihuahuas were crossed with the enchanting little Toy Spaniel, or Comforter as it was then called, that has been depicted by many famous artists.

Paintings of these toy dogs can be seen in galleries throughout Europe. This crossbreeding, moreover, probably produced the beautiful little butterfly dog, the Papillon, which in turn was taken centuries later to the USA, where in the 20th century it was crossed with the Smooth Coat Chihuahua to help produce the Long Coat variety.

GROOMING

Chihuahuas are easy dogs to groom. If a drop or two of linseed or wheat germ oil for dogs is added to the diet, a glorious, glossy sheen will soon be acquired. Smooth Coats require extraordinarily little attention. A few minutes daily is enough, while the Long Coats take just a little longer. Once a month, however, the dogs need a thorough going-over with a little added attention. The first of each month, or first Sunday, is a good time to set aside for this. The weeks go by so quickly that the monthly grooming can be easily forgotten. The inside of the ears should be examined to make sure that they are clean. The tips of the ears sometimes become clogged with grease and dead hair if they have been overlooked in the daily grooming. The teeth should be looked over carefully to see if there are any signs of tartar, which is like a yellow scale at the base of the teeth. Tartar can be removed with a special dog tooth scaler. When the dog chews hard biscuits or chew pacifiers, such as Nylabone® products, he removes the tartar himself. The nails grow long quickly and should be kept short with special clippers. Whiskers, if they are to be kept short, will need constant trimming.

Even the Long Coat Chihuahua is remarkably easy to groom. Little more than a daily brushing is necessary to keep the coat clean and healthy.

EQUIPMENT

A good, hard, bristle brush or a soft, nylon brush is essential. A fine comb is also useful when grooming a Long Coat. Talcum powder is good for cleaning the coat and for keeping the dogs smelling fresh and sweet. Normal saline solution made by adding a tiny bit of salt to boiled water is useful for cleaning the eyes if they become runny and stained. A silk handkerchief is wonderful for rubbing over the coat after brushing to make it glossy. Good nail clippers (the guillotine type is the easiest to use) are absolutely essential, as some Chihuahuas grow very long nails. Curved

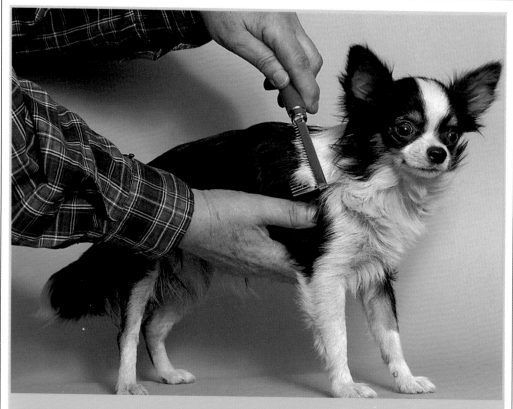

Your Chihuahua will appreciate a daily grooming session, even if it takes only a few minutes. Comb through the neck and body in both directions, always ending up by combing the way the hair grows.

surgical scissors are useful if the whiskers are to be kept short, and for cutting the long hair which grows between the pads of the feet in the Long Coat Chihuahua. A can of flea powder should be kept for use when necessary. A flea collar can be worn if fleas are prevalent. Boric acid is excellent if the hair below the eyes gets stained. Coconut oil is useful for growing hair, and for cleaning the tips of the ears. A good coconut oil shampoo keeps the coat clean and glossy, but Chihuahuas do not really require bathing more than twice a year, unless, of course, they are being exhibited.

WHEN TO GROOM

There is no doubt that all dogs look better and fresher if they are groomed every day. This need not take more than a few moments and it is well worthwhile to keep the Chihuahua looking his smartest at all times, ready for admiration. Besides the regular grooming routine, a Chihuahua that is not feeling up to par should be brushed carefully once or twice a day. It is good for morale and makes him feel cared for and fresh.

BRUSHING

Since a Chihuahua is so tiny,

he must be groomed gently. This is best done by standing him on a table covered with newspaper. Since Chihuahuas have large eyes, great care must be taken when brushing, so if the dog turns his head suddenly, the bristles will not damage an eye. The ears are tender and most dogs do not like having them touched. It is important, however, to brush the ears gently, particularly the edges, both inside and outside. The neck and body should be well brushed both ways, always ending up by brushing the way the hair grows. The tail, which ought to be wide and flat, has more hair than any other area and it should be brushed carefully.

Occasionally, a dog that lies on a hard surface will rub the top of his tail, making a ridge which becomes hairless. If this area is massaged gently with a softening

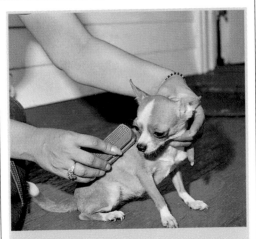

Because of the tiny size and fragility of your Chihuahua, you must be very gentle when grooming. His eyes are very large and can be easily damaged by the bristles of a brush if you are not careful.

cream, the hair will start growing again. If the skin is permitted to remain hard, this area of the tail will often be bald. Some Chihuahuas suffer from a small bald patch on the throat. Coconut oil rubbed on frequently will usually help hair to grow, and in time the patch will probably disappear, but it is nothing to worry about.

CARE OF THE EYES

Most Chihuahuas' eyes require little or no attention. There are, however, some dogs that have the misfortune to suffer from watering eyes, especially when they are in the wind. This sometimes leads to an ugly orange stain beneath the eyes, and dark crusts form below them. In these cases the eyes should be rinsed with normal saline solution at body temperature. The rims should be

All kinds of brushes, combs, and other types of grooming tools are available to the Chihuahua owner. See your local pet shop to find the tools you need. Photo courtesy of The Kong Company.

washed carefully removing any crust that has formed. Dry the area well with cotton pads. The stain is often difficult to remove, but boric acid, applied carefully to the area, dries up the dampness and helps to remove it.

Prevention is easier than cure, and the eyes should be wiped with a clean cotton pad whenever they are runny. Chihuahuas, being near the ground, are apt to get more dust in their eyes than do taller dogs and do come into contact with drafts more often. The stain or crust is unsightly and uncomfortable. It should be attended to immediately and as often as necessary, and the dog

Carefully inspect the ears for evidence of any dirt accumulation or parasites. To keep your Chihuahua comfortable and to prevent infection, a cotton swab can be used to clean away any soap, dirt, or grease residue from the inside of the ears.

should be kept out of drafts and chilling winds.

CARE OF THE EARS

Ears are often overlooked in the general grooming, and this is liable to cause an accumulation of dead scurf, old hair and grease, which sometimes appears as a hard dark brown edge on the ears that can be very uncomfortable. If they are in this state, do not try to pull the dead hair out as this will only make them sore and perhaps cause them to bleed. It is better to massage the tips with a little almond oil or coconut oil to soften the crust. Then wash them with a good coconut oil shampoo, rubbing the tips gently and easing away the dead, loose hair. If the crust is very resistant, a soft nail brush can be used, but care must be taken not to make the ears sore by rubbing too

Do not overlook the ears when grooming your Chihuahua. Wash them with a good shampoo and afterward remove all water from the inside with a cotton swab.

hard. Rinse them thoroughly several times. They must be dried gently, particularly deep inside, in case any water has penetrated there. If, after the removal of the dead hair, the skin looks dry and scaly, rub on a little coconut oil for two or three days.

If the ears have been neglected for some time, they may look bald or even moth-eaten on the edges. It is better to get the dead hair out, because the sooner it is removed the faster the new hair will come in. Hair generally takes about five weeks to grow, but with regular grooming, clogging of the ears should happen only rarely.

Some Chihuahuas produce ear wax in their ears. To deal with this, use a cotton-tipped swab. With the help of someone to hold the dog, lift the tip of the ear

Your Chihuahua will need to have his nails clipped regularly. Your dog will be nervous at first, but after a few trimmings he will grow used to his paws' being handled and trimmed.

upwards with the thumb and finger of the left hand and gently twist the cotton swab into the orifice of the ear. Keep using

Smooth Coat Chihuahuas are never trimmed, however occasionally they may need to have their whiskers trimmed. When doing so, be very careful not to inadvertently poke your Chihuahua in his vulnerable eyes.

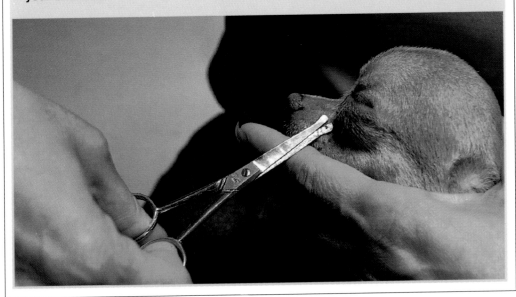

fresh swabs until the ear is clean. Since the ear is delicate, do not dig down too deeply, and take great care not to hurt the dog or damage the ear.

If the dog continually scratches around his ear, check for any sign of mites. If none are

coated dogs will grow thick and long hairs between the pads of their feet. This makes the pads spread out. Once a month this hair should be trimmed with blunt-ended scissors, taking care not to nip the pads. If the hair grows very long, trim it to the

Any stain or crust that appears in the corners of your Chihuahua's eyes should be gently wiped away with a cotton swab wet with warm water. The stain or crust is unsightly and uncomfortable and should be attended to immediately.

found, and the scratching continues, take the dog to the veterinarian for a further check-up.

COAT TRIMMING

Smooth Coat Chihuahuas are never trimmed. Long Coats require the excess hair which grows between their pads to be trimmed occasionally. Heavily

edge of the toenails. Do not trim it above the toenail, as this spoils the shape of the foot. Long hair at the back of the pad can also be trimmed to ground length, if necessary, or to the edge of the pad, whichever looks better. Since dogs are ticklish between their toes, it is easier to trim the pads with the help of a second person.

The teeth should be looked over carefully to see if there are any signs of tartar, which is like a yellow scale at the base of the teeth.

BATHING

Well-groomed dogs require bathing only about twice a year as too many baths remove the natural oils from the coat, and the dogs get dirtier faster. For the Long Coats an occasional extra wash of the tail and feathers, and perhaps the ruff, if it gets dirty, is sufficient.

To bathe a Chihuahua, first assemble everything needed for the operation. Use a good coconut oil shampoo or a suitable dog shampoo. Have a large warm towel and a chamois skin for drying, kept solely for this purpose. A jar of petroleum jelly for smearing around the rims of the eyes to keep the soap out, a washcloth for the face, and some cotton to plug the ears to prevent the water from going in are also required. If there is a rubber spray to attach to the faucet, so much the better, as spraying helps get the soap out of the coat. Finally, some method for quick drying is desirable, such as a hair dryer.

The easiest place to bathe a Chihuahua is probably the kitchen sink. Use two bowls of warm water. Dogs do not like hot water and some hate being bathed; so talk to your Chihuahua in a quiet, encouraging voice as you smear a little petroleum jelly around the eye rims, and plug each ear with a large puff of cotton. Then, stand the dog in one bowl and wet the coat all over. Pour a little shampoo on the hand, wash

Immediately after your Chihuahua is finished with his bath, wrap him in a towel to keep him warm and wipe the petroleum jelly away from his eyes.

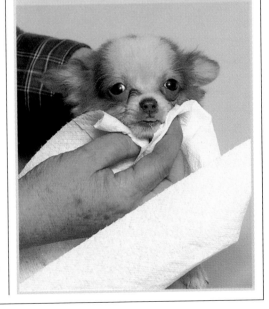

carefully all around the head and neck, paying particular attention to the edges of the ears.

Next, rub the soap all over the body and the tail, including, of course, the trousers and the belly. Gently massage each leg and foot. After a good lather has been worked up, spray the dog with warm water, or place him in the clean bowl. Rinse thoroughly, taking care that the water and soap do not get into his eyes. Repeat the shampooing and rinse three times. If a spray is not available, it is a good idea to have two jugs of warm water waiting, so that after the first rinse with one jug of water, the dog can be put into the second bowl for the remains of the soap to be rinsed off, and then given a final rinse from the second jug.

Pick the dog up gently, put him on the floor and allow him to shake himself. Remove the cotton from his ears if he has not already shaken it out, wrap him in a warm towel, and wipe the petroleum jelly off the eyes. Give him a quick rub over with the towel, then dry him, using the hair dryer on warm heat. From then on wipe him down with the clean chamois, using long clean strokes. The chamois skin will dry the dog much more quickly than any towel. Check the ears, and do not let the dog out until he is thoroughly dry all over. In cold weather it is wise not to let him out again, even to relieve himself. Dogs can easily catch a chill, particularly after being wet and sitting in front of a warm fire. Keep him away from drafts. When he is thoroughly dry, he can be given a good brushing and a gentle combing if he is a Long Coat.

Chihuahuas love to wear sweaters. After a bath, putting a soft warm sweater on your Chihuahua will keep him from catching a chill.

Finally, finish off by drawing a silk scarf over the coat the way the hair grows. This brings up a glorious sheen.

Baths during inclement weather can, of course, be given with one of the dry shampoos available in pet shops.

YOUR NEW CHIHUAHUA PUPPY

SELECTION

When you do pick out a Chihuahua puppy as a pet, don't be hasty; the longer you study puppies, the better you will understand them. Make it your transcendent concern to select retreat to his bed or his box, or plays coy behind other puppies or people, or hides his head under your arm or jacket appealing to your protective instinct. *Pick the Chihuahua*

When choosing a Chihuahua, don't be hasty. The more you study different specimens of the breed, the better you will understand them and the easier your decision will be.

only one that radiates good health and spirit and is lively on his feet, whose eyes are bright, whose coat shines, and who comes forward eagerly to make and to cultivate your acquaintance. Don't fall for any shy little darling that wants to *puppy who forthrightly picks you! The feeling of attraction should be mutual!*

DOCUMENTS

Now, a little paper work is in order. When you purchase a purebred Chihuahua puppy, you should receive a transfer of ownership, registration material, and other "papers" (a list of the immunization shots, if any, the puppy may have been given; a note on whether or not the puppy has been wormed; a diet and

have chosen it very carefully over all other breeds and all other puppies. So before you ever get that Chihuahua puppy home, you will have prepared for its arrival by reading everything you can get your hands on having to do with

As shown by these Chihuahua pups, a persistent playful attitude prevails with the breed.

feeding schedule to which the puppy is accustomed) and you are welcomed as a fellow owner to a long, pleasant association with a most lovable pet, and more (news)paper work.

GENERAL PREPARATION

You have chosen to own a particular Chihuahua puppy. You

the management of Chihuahuas and puppies. True, you will run into many conflicting opinions, but at least you will not be starting "blind." Read, study, digest. Talk over your plans with your veterinarian, other "Chihuahua people," and the seller of your Chihuahua puppy.

When you get your Chihuahua

At eight weeks of age, a Chihuahua puppy weighs about one-half pound. When selecting dogs, owners should avoid excessive smallness, as these dogs are more prone to health problems.

Chihuahua puppies are tiny and fragile and must be handled with extreme care. Let the breeder show you how to properly handle a puppy.

carton lined with newspapers provides protection for puppy and car, if you are driving alone. Avoid excitement and unnecessary handling of the puppy on arrival. A Chihuahua puppy is a very small "package" to be making a complete change of surroundings and company, and he needs frequent rest and refreshment to renew his vitality.

THE FIRST DAY AND NIGHT

When your Chihuahua puppy arrives in your home, put him down on the floor and don't pick him up again, except when it is absolutely necessary. He is a dog, a real dog, and must not be lugged around like a rag doll.

puppy, you will find that your reading and study are far from finished. You've just scratched the surface in your plan to provide the greatest possible comfort and health for your Chihuahua; and, by the same token, you do want to assure yourself of the greatest possible enjoyment of this wonderful creature. You must be ready for this puppy mentally as well as in the physical requirements.

TRANSPORTATION

If you take the puppy home by car, protect him from drafts, particularly in cold weather. Wrapped in a towel and carried in the arms or lap of a passenger, the Chihuahua puppy will usually make the trip without mishap. If the pup starts to drool and to squirm, stop the car for a few minutes. Have newspapers handy in case of car-sickness. A covered

A wire crate like this one is a wise purchase. It will come in handy for traveling with your dog. If you buy one when you first acquire your Chihuahua puppy, you will be able to use it through his adulthood.

Handle him as little as possible, and permit no one to pick him up and baby him. To repeat, *put your Chihuahua puppy on the floor or the ground and let him stay there except when it may be necessary to do otherwise.*

Quite possibly your Chihuahua puppy will be afraid for a while in his new surroundings, without his mother and littermates. Comfort him and reassure him, but don't console him. Don't give him the "oh-you-poor-itsy-bitsy-puppy" treatment. Be calm, friendly, and reassuring. Encourage him to walk around and sniff over his new home. If it's dark, put on the lights. Let him roam for a few minutes while you and everyone else concerned sit quietly or go about your routine business. Let the puppy come back to you.

When you first bring your Chihuahua puppy home he will be very excited. Give him time to become used to his new surroundings.

Chihuahua puppies should be outgoing, alert and curious. Shyness and nervousness can lead to serious problems later in life.

Playmates may cause an immediate problem if the new Chihuahua puppy is to be greeted by children or other pets. If not, you can skip this subject. The natural affinity between puppies and children calls for some supervision until a live-and-let-live relationship is established. This applies particularly to a Christmas puppy, when there is more excitement than usual and more chance for a puppy to swallow something upsetting. It is a better plan to welcome the puppy several days before or after the holiday week. Like a baby, your Chihuahua puppy needs much rest and should not be over-handled. Once a child realizes that a puppy has "feelings" similar to his own, and can readily be hurt or injured, the opportunities for play and responsibilities provide exercise and training for both.

For his first night with you,

The whole family, including the children, should be involved in the process of selecting a Chihuahua puppy. It seems that this young lady has made her choice!

he should be put where he is to sleep every night—say in the kitchen, since its floor can usually be easily cleaned. Let him explore the kitchen to his heart's content; close doors to confine him there. Prepare his food and feed him lightly the first night. Give him a pan with some water in it—not a lot, since most puppies will try to drink the whole pan dry. Give him an old coat or shirt to lie on. Since a coat or shirt will be strong in human scent, he will pick it out to lie on, thus furthering his feeling of security in the room where he has just been fed.

HOUSEBREAKING HELPS

Now, sooner or later—mostly sooner—your new Chihuahua puppy is going to "puddle" on the floor. First take a newspaper and lay it on the puddle until the urine is soaked up onto the paper. *Save this paper.* Now take a cloth with soap and water, wipe up the floor and dry it well. Then take the wet paper and place it on a fairly large square of newspapers in a convenient corner. When cleaning up, always keep a piece of wet paper on top of the others. Every time he wants to "squat," he will seek out this spot and use the papers. (This routine is rarely necessary for more than three days.) Now leave your Chihuahua puppy for the night. Quite probably he will cry and howl a bit; some are more stubborn than others on this matter. But let him stay alone for the night. This may seem harsh treatment, but it is the best procedure in the long run. Just let him cry; he will weary of it sooner or later.

To avoid a yappy, aggressive adult, socializing your Chihuahua with other dogs is advisable at a young age.

The Chihuahua is a graceful, alert, swift-moving little dog with a saucy expression.

THE CHIHUAHUA STANDARD

A breed standard is the criterion by which the appearance (and to a certain extent, the temperament as well) of any given dog is made subject to objective measurement. Basically, the standard for any breed is a definition of the perfect dog to which all specimens of the breed are compared. Breed standards are always subject to change through review by the national breed club for each dog, so that it is always wise to keep up with developments in a breed by checking the publications of your national kennel club. Printed below is the American Kennel Club standard for the Chihuahua.

On the Smooth Coat Chihuahua the coat should be more sparse on the head and ears than on the rest of the body, with a ruff on the neck preferred.

General Appearance—A graceful, alert, swift-moving little dog with saucy expression, compact, and with terrier-like qualities of temperament.

Size, Proportion, Substance— **Weight**—A well balanced little dog not to exceed 6 pounds. **Proportion**—The body is off-square; hence, slightly longer when measured from point of shoulder to point of buttocks than height at the withers. Somewhat shorter bodies are preferred in males. Disqualification—Any dog over 6 pounds in weight.

Head—A well rounded "apple dome" skull, with or without molera. **Expression**— Saucy. **Eyes**— Full, but not protruding, balanced, set well apart— luminous dark or luminous ruby. (Light eyes in blond or white-colored dogs permissible.) **Ears**—Large, erect type ears, held more upright when alert, but flaring to the sides at a 45 degree angle when in repose, giving breadth between the ears. **Muzzle**— Moderately short, slightly pointed. Cheeks and jaws lean. **Nose**—Self-colored in blond types, or black. In moles, blues, and chocolates, they are self-colored. In blond types, pink nose permissible. **Bite**—Level or scissors. Overshot or undershot

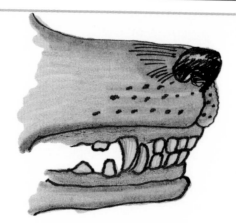

Scissors Bite

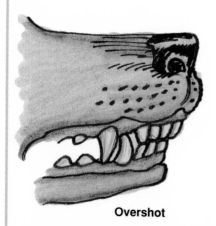

Overshot

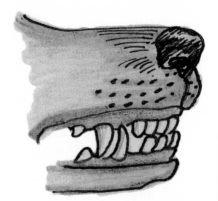

Undershot

The Chihuahua should have a level or scissors bite. Overshot or undershot bite, or any distortion of the bite or jaw is a serious fault. Drawings by John Quinn.

bite, or any distortion of the bite or jaw, should be penalized as a serious fault. *Disqualifications*—Broken down or cropped ears.

Neck, Topline, Body—*Neck*—Slightly arched, gracefully sloping into lean shoulders. *Topline*—Level. *Body*—Ribs rounded and well sprung (but not too much "barrel-shaped"). *Tail*—Moderately long, carried sickle either up or out, or in a loop over the back, with tip just touching the back. (Never tucked between legs.)
Disqualifications—Cropped tail, bobtail.

Forequarters—Shoulders—Lean, sloping into a slightly broadening support above straight forelegs that set well under, giving a free play at the elbows. Shoulders should be well up, giving balance and soundness, sloping into a level back. (Never down or low.) This gives a chestiness, and strength of forequarters, yet not of the

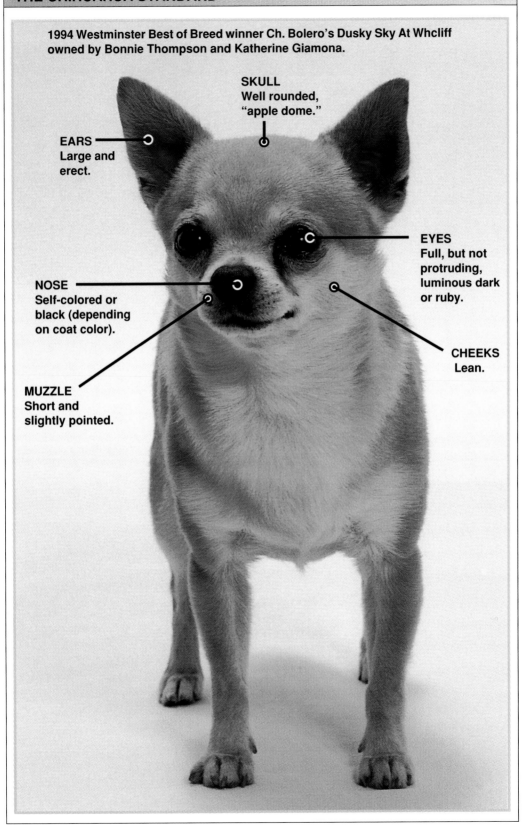

1994 Westminster Best of Breed winner Ch. Bolero's Dusky Sky At Whcliff owned by Bonnie Thompson and Katherine Giamona.

SKULL
Well rounded, "apple dome."

EARS
Large and erect.

EYES
Full, but not protruding, luminous dark or ruby.

NOSE
Self-colored or black (depending on coat color).

CHEEKS
Lean.

MUZZLE
Short and slightly pointed.

Above: The Smooth Coat Chihuahua's coat should be of soft texture, close and glossy. The hair on the tail is preferred furry.

Below: The Long Coat Chihuahua should have a coat that is of a soft texture, either flat or slightly curly. The tail should be full and long, as a plume.

The correct angle of ear placement.

Good type Smooth Coat head.

Good type Long Coat head.

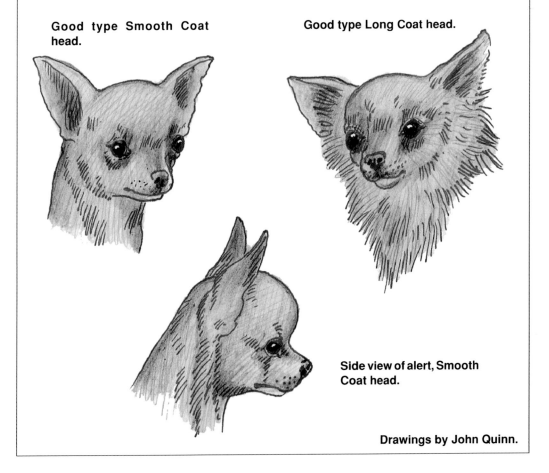

Side view of alert, Smooth Coat head.

Drawings by John Quinn.

"Bulldog" chest. *Feet*—A small, dainty foot with toes well split up but not spread, pads cushioned. (Neither the hare nor the cat foot.) *Pasterns*—Fine.

Hindquarters—Muscular, with hocks well apart, neither out nor in, well let down, firm and sturdy. The feet are as in front.

Coat—In the Smooth Coats, the coat should be of soft texture, close and glossy. (Heavier coats with undercoats permissible.) Coat placed well over body with ruff on neck preferred, and more scanty on head and ears. Hair on tail preferred furry. In Long Coats, the coat should be of a soft texture, either flat or slightly curly, with undercoat preferred. *Ears*—Fringed. (Heavily fringed ears may be tipped slightly if due to the fringes and not to weak ear leather, never down.) *Tail*—Full and long (as a plume). Feathering on feet and legs, pants on hind legs and large ruff on the neck desired and preferred. *Disqualification*—In

The ears of the Long Coat Chihuahua should be fringed, and a large ruff on the neck is desired and preferred.

Long Coats, too thin coat that resembles bareness.

Color—Any color—Solid, marked or splashed.

Gait—The Chihuahua should move swiftly with a firm, sturdy action, with good reach in front equal to the drive from the rear. From the rear, the hocks remain parallel to each other, and the foot fall of the rear legs follows directly behind that of the forelegs. The legs, both front and rear, will tend to converge slightly toward a central line of gravity as speed increases. The side view shows good, strong drive in the rear and plenty of reach in the front, with head carried high. The topline should remain firm and the backline level as the dog moves.

Temperament—Alert, with terrier-like qualities.

Disqualifications: Any dog over 6 pounds in weight. Broken down or cropped ears. Cropped tail, bobtail. In Long Coats, too thin coat that resembles bareness.

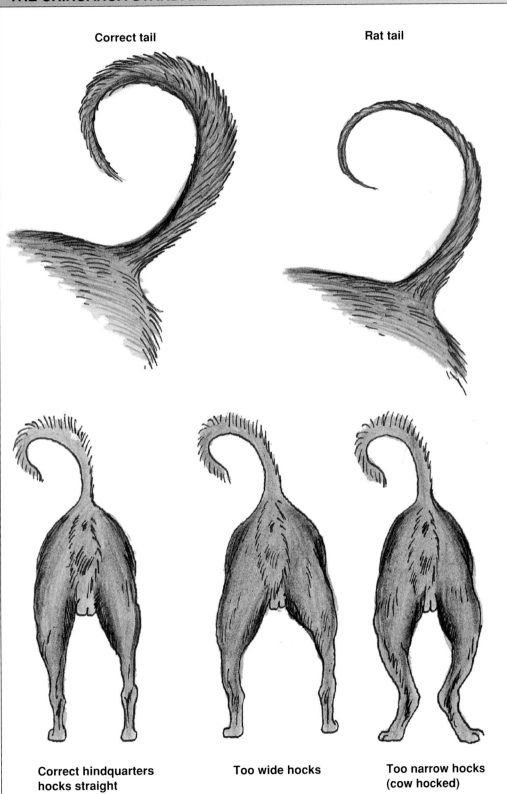

Correct tail

Rat tail

Correct hindquarters
hocks straight

Too wide hocks

Too narrow hocks
(cow hocked)

Drawings by John Quinn.

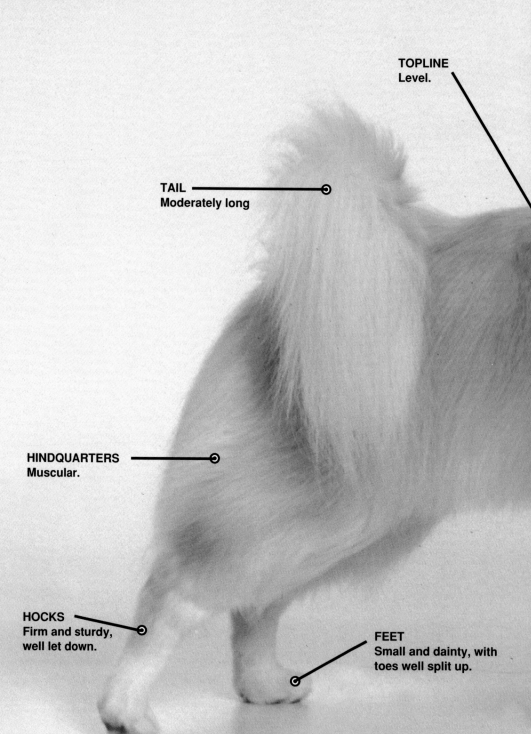

1995 Westminster Best of Breed Long Coat Chihuahua Ch. Simpatica Celeste owned by Mrs. Keith Thomas.

TOPLINE
Level.

TAIL
Moderately long

HINDQUARTERS
Muscular.

HOCKS
Firm and sturdy,
well let down.

FEET
Small and dainty, with
toes well split up.

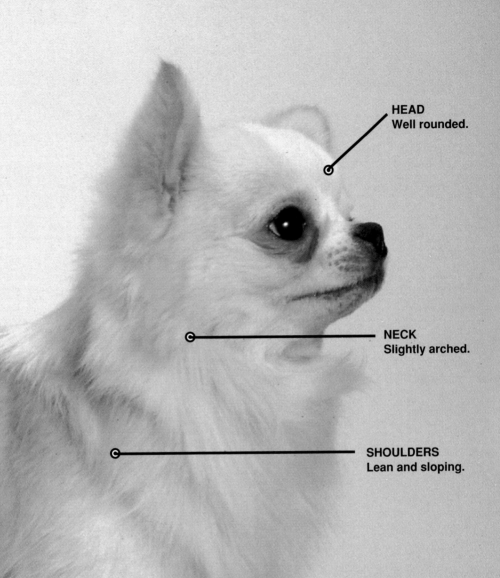

HEAD
Well rounded.

NECK
Slightly arched.

SHOULDERS
Lean and sloping.

FORELEGS
Set well under.

PASTERNS
Fine.

FEEDING

Now let's talk about feeding your Chihuahua, a subject so simple that it's amazing there is so much nonsense and misunderstanding about it. Is it expensive to feed a Chihuahua? No, it is not! You can feed your Chihuahua economically and keep him in perfect shape the year round, or you can feed him expensively. He'll thrive either way, and let's see why this is true.

First of all, remember a Chihuahua is a dog. Dogs do not have a high degree of selectivity in their food, and unless you spoil them with great variety (and possibly

Like most dogs, a Chihuahua can be fed very simply and inexpensively. Variety is not really necessary unless you choose to spoil your dog, in which case you will wind up with a picky eater.

turn them into poor, "picky" eaters) they will eat almost anything that they become accustomed to. Many dogs flatly refuse to eat nice, fresh beef. They pick around it and eat everything else. But meat—bah! Why? They aren't accustomed to it! They'd eat rabbit fast enough, but

they refuse beef because they aren't used to it.

VARIETY NOT NECESSARY

A good general rule of thumb is forget all human preferences and don't give a thought to variety. Choose the right diet for your Chihuahua and feed it to him day after day, year after year, winter and summer. But what is the right diet?

Hundreds of thousands of dollars have been spent in canine nutrition research. The results are pretty conclusive, so you needn't go into a lot of experimenting with trials of this and that every other week. Research has proven just what your dog needs to eat and to keep healthy.

DOG FOOD

There are almost as many right diets as there are dog experts, but the basic diet most often recommended is one that consists

The diet most recommended for dogs consists of a dry food or kibble. Your best bet is to stick with a well-known brand, as they probably have spent much time and money on research and testing.

of a dry food, either meal or kibble form. There are several of excellent quality, manufactured by reliable companies, research tested, and nationally advertised. They are inexpensive, highly satisfactory, and easily available in stores everywhere in containers of five to 50 pounds. Larger amounts cost less per pound, usually.

If you have a choice of brands, it is usually safer to choose the better known one; but even so, carefully read the analysis on the package. Do not choose any food in which the protein level is less than 25 percent, and be sure that this protein comes from both animal and vegetable sources. The good dog foods have meat meal, fish meal, liver, and such, plus protein from alfalfa and soy beans, as well as some dried-milk product. Note the vitamin content carefully. See that they are all there in good proportions; and be especially certain that the food contains properly high levels of vitamins A and D, two of the most perishable and important ones. Note the B-complex level, but don't worry about carbohydrate and mineral levels. These substances are plentiful and cheap and not likely to be lacking in a good brand.

The advice given for how to choose a dry food also applies to moist or canned types of dog foods, if you decide to feed one of these.

Having chosen a really good food, feed it to your Chihuahua as the manufacturer directs. And once you've started, stick to it. Never change if you can possibly help it. A switch from one meal or kibble-type food can usually be made without too much upset; however, a change will almost invariably give you (and your Chihuahua) some trouble.

is having puppies. Vitamins and minerals are naturally present in all the foods; and to ensure against any loss through processing, they are added in concentrated form to the dog food you use. Except on the advice of your veterinarian,

This hungry Chihuahua finds his meal good to the last drop!

WHEN SUPPLEMENTS ARE NEEDED

Now what about supplements of various kinds, mineral and vitamin, or the various oils? They are all okay to add to your Chihuahua's food. However, if you are feeding your Chihuahua a correct diet, and this is easy to do, no supplements are necessary unless your Chihuahua has been improperly fed, has been sick, or

added amounts of vitamins can prove harmful to your Chihuahua! The same risk goes with minerals.

FEEDING SCHEDULE

When and how much food to give your Chihuahua? As to when (except in the instance of puppies), suit yourself. You may feed two meals per day or the same amount in one single feeding, either morning or night. As to how to prepare the food and how much to give, it is generally best to follow the directions on the food package. Your own Chihuahua may want a little more or a little less.

Fresh, cool water should always be available to your Chihuahua. This is important to good health throughout his lifetime.

ALL CHIHUAHUAS NEED TO CHEW

Puppies and young Chihuahuas need something with resistance to chew on while their teeth and jaws are developing—for cutting the puppy teeth, to induce growth of the permanent teeth under the puppy teeth, to assist in getting rid of the puppy teeth at the proper time, to help the permanent teeth through the gums, to ensure normal jaw

Sometimes your Chihuahua may need supplementation to his regular diet. Usually vitamin supplements can be mixed in with food or administered orally.

development, and to settle the permanent teeth solidly in the jaws.

Always provide your Chihuahua with fresh, cool water. It is the most important and least expensive component in his diet, so supply it freely.

The adult Chihuahua's desire to chew stems from the instinct for tooth cleaning, gum massage, and jaw exercise—plus the need for an outlet for periodic doggie tensions.

This is why dogs, especially puppies and young dogs, will often destroy property worth hundreds of dollars when their chewing instinct is not diverted from their owner's possessions. And this is why you should provide your Chihuahua with something to chew— something that has the necessary

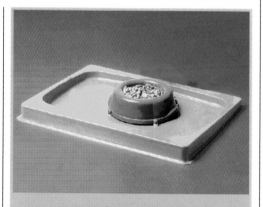

For no-mess feeding, a feeding tray is very practical. Feeding trays are available in different styles and colors at your local pet shop. Photo courtesy of Penn Plax.

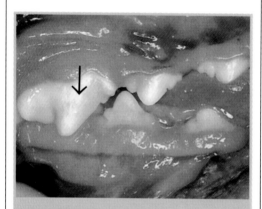

In a scientific study, this shows a dog's tooth (arrow) while being maintained by Gumabone® chewing.

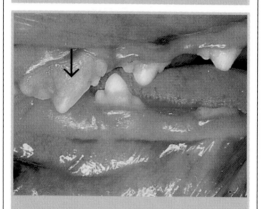

The Gumabone® was taken away and in 30 days the tooth was almost completely covered with plaque and tartar.

functional qualities, is desirable from the Chihuahua's viewpoint, and is safe for him.

It is very important that your Chihuahua not be permitted to chew on anything he can break or on any indigestible thing from which he can bite sizable chunks. Sharp pieces, such as from a bone which can be broken by a dog, may pierce the intestinal wall and kill. Indigestible things that can be bitten off in chunks, such as from shoes or rubber or plastic toys, may cause an intestinal stoppage (if not regurgitated) and bring painful death, unless surgery is promptly performed.

Strong natural bones, such as 4- to 8-inch lengths of round shin bone from mature beef—either the kind you can get from a butcher or one of the variety available commercially in pet stores—may serve your Chihuahua's teething needs if his mouth is large enough to handle them effectively. You may be tempted to give your Chihuahua puppy a smaller bone and he may not be able to break it when you do, but puppies grow rapidly and the power of their jaws constantly increases until maturity. This means that a growing Chihuahua may break one of the smaller bones at any time, swallow the up and swallowed by your Chihuahua provide little, if any, usable calcium or other nutriment. They do, however, disturb the digestion of most dogs and cause them to vomit the nourishing food they need.

Dried rawhide products of

Nylafloss® attracts dogs and keeps them busy for hours. In addition to being a safe and fun chew toy, Nylafloss® is very healthy for your Chihuahua, since its primary function is a doggy dental floss.

pieces, and die painfully before you realize what is wrong.

All hard natural bones are very abrasive. If your Chihuahua is an avid chewer, natural bones may wear away his teeth prematurely; hence, they then should be taken away from your dog when the teething purposes have been served. The badly worn, and usually painful, teeth of many mature dogs can be traced to excessive chewing on natural bones.

Contrary to popular belief, knuckle bones that can be chewed various types, shapes, sizes, and prices are available on the market and have become quite popular. However, they don't serve the primary chewing functions very well; they are a bit messy when wet from mouthing, and most Chihuahuas chew them up rather rapidly—but they have been considered safe for dogs until recently. Now, more and more incidents of death, and near death, by strangulation have been reported to be the results of partially swallowed chunks of rawhide swelling in the throat.

The hambone-scented Gumabone® Pooch Pacifier is a safe, flavorful, and effective chewing device. The "petite" size is ideal for the Chihuahua.

More recently, some veterinarians have been attributing cases of acute constipation to large pieces of incompletely digested rawhide in the intestine.

A new product, molded rawhide, is very safe. During the process, the rawhide is melted and then injection molded into the familiar dog shape. It is very hard and is eagerly accepted by Chihuahuas. The melting process also sterilizes the rawhide. Don't confuse this with pressed rawhide, which is nothing more than small strips of rawhide squeezed together.

The nylon bones, especially those with natural meat and bone fractions added, are probably the most complete, safe, and economical answer to the chewing need. Dogs cannot break them or bite off sizable chunks; hence, they are completely safe—and being longer lasting than other things offered for the purpose, they are economical.

Hard chewing raises little bristle-like projections on the surface of the nylon bones—to provide effective interim tooth cleaning and vigorous gum massage, much in the same way your toothbrush does it for you. The little projections are raked off and swallowed in the form of thin shavings, but the chemistry of the nylon is such that they break down in the stomach fluids and pass through without effect.

The toughness of the nylon provides the strong chewing resistance needed for important jaw exercise and effectively aids teething functions, but there is no tooth wear because nylon is non-abrasive. Being inert, nylon does not support the growth of microorganisms; and it can be washed in soap and water or it can be sterilized by boiling or in an autoclave.

Nylabone® is highly recommended by veterinarians as a safe, healthy nylon bone that can't splinter or chip. Nylabone® is frizzled by the dog's chewing action, creating a toothbrush-like surface that cleanses the teeth and massages the gums. Nylabone®, the only chew products made of flavor-impregnated solid nylon, are available in your local pet shop. Nylabone® is superior to the cheaper bones because it is made of virgin nylon, which is the strongest and longest-lasting type of nylon available. The cheaper bones are made from recycled or re-ground nylon scraps, and have a tendency to break apart and split easily.

Nothing, however, substitutes for periodic professional attention for your Chihuahua's teeth and gums, not any more than your toothbrush can do that for you. Have your Chihuahua's teeth cleaned at least once a year by your veterinarian (twice a year is better) and he will be happier, healthier, and far more pleasant to live with.

It is natural for all dogs to chew as a means to release doggy tensions. If you don't provide your dog with a safe and healthy chew toy, he's likely to chew on your possessions. This Chihuahua is being introduced to the Gumabone® Wishbone®, an excellent alternative to his owner's new shoes!

Molded rawhide is the safest alternative to the sometimes dangerous dried rawhide products. Do not confuse high-quality molded rawhide products such as Roar-Hide™ with pressed rawhide, which is nothing more than a cheap imitation.

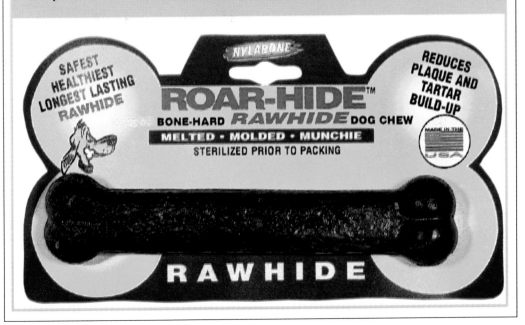

TRAINING

You owe proper training to your Chihuahua. The right and privilege of being trained is his birthright; and whether your Chihuahua is going to be a handsome, well-mannered housedog and companion, a show dog, or whatever possible use he may be put to, the basic training is always the same—all must start with basic obedience, or what might be called "manner training."

Your Chihuahua must come instantly when called and obey the "Sit" or "Down" command just as fast; he must walk quietly at "Heel," whether on or off lead. He must be mannerly and polite wherever he goes; he must be polite to strangers on the street and in stores. He must be mannerly in the presence of other dogs. He must not bark at children on roller skates, motorcycles, or other domestic animals. And he must be restrained from chasing cats. It is not a dog's inalienable right to chase cats, and he must be reprimanded for it.

Training is a responsibility you owe to your Chihuahua. Besides being special bonding times with your pal, training sessions could one day save your Chihuahua's life.

PROFESSIONAL TRAINING

How do you go about this training? Well, it's a very simple procedure, pretty well standardized by now. First, if you can afford the extra expense, you may send your Chihuahua to a professional trainer, where in 30 to 60 days he will learn how to be a "good dog." If you enlist the services of a good professional trainer, follow his advice of when to come to see the dog. No, he won't forget you, but too-frequent visits at the wrong time may slow down his training progress. And using a "pro" trainer means that you will have to go for some training, too, after the trainer feels your Chihuahua is ready to go home. You will have to learn how your Chihuahua works, just what to expect of him and how to use what the dog has learned after he is home.

Despite its size, the Chihuahua is very athletic and capable of learning many tricks.

OBEDIENCE TRAINING CLASS

Another way to train your Chihuahua (many experienced Chihuahua people think this is the best) is to join an obedience training class right in your own community. There is such a group in nearly every community nowadays. Here you will be working with a group of people who are also just starting out. You will actually be training your own dog, since all work is done under the direction of a head trainer who will make suggestions to you and also tell you when and how to correct your Chihuahua's errors. Then, too, working with such a group, your Chihuahua will learn to get along with other dogs. And, what is more important, he will learn to do exactly what he is told to do, no matter how much confusion there is around him or how great the temptation is to go his own way.

Write to your national kennel club for the location of a training club or class in your locality. Sign up. Go to it regularly—every session! Go early and leave late! Both you and your Chihuahua will benefit tremendously.

Jumping up on people is an annoying habit for a dog to acquire. Train your Chihuahua from puppyhood to not jump on people—your well-dressed guests will appreciate it.

TRAIN HIM BY THE BOOK

The third way of training your Chihuahua is by the book. Yes, you can do it this way and do a good job of it too. But in using the book method, select a book, buy it, study it carefully; then study it some more, until the procedures are almost second nature to you. Then start your training. But stay with the book and its advice and exercises. Don't start in and then make up a few rules of your own. If you don't follow the book, you'll get into jams you can't get out of by yourself. If after a few hours of short training sessions your Chihuahua is still not working as he should, get back to the book for a study session, because it's your fault, not the dog's! The procedures of dog training have been so well systemized that it must be your fault, since literally thousands of fine Chihuahuas have been trained by the book.

After your Chihuahua is "letter perfect" under all conditions, then, if you wish, go on to advanced training and trick work.

Your Chihuahua will love his obedience training, and you'll burst with pride at the finished product! Your Chihuahua will enjoy life even more, and you'll enjoy your Chihuahua more. And remember—you *owe good training to your Chihuahua.*

YOUR CHIHUAHUA'S HEALTH

We know our pets, their moods and habits, and therefore we can recognize when our Chihuahua is experiencing an off-day. Signs of sickness can be very obvious or very subtle. As any mother can you respect. Visit more than one vet before you make a lifelong choice. Trust your instincts. Find a knowledgeable, compassionate vet who knows Chihuahuas and likes them.

Daily outdoor exercise, proper diet, and regular visits to the veterinarian are the essentials of a long-lived Chihuahua.

attest, diagnosing and treating an ailment requires common sense, knowing when to seek home remedies and when to visit your doctor...or veterinarian, as the case may be.

Your veterinarian, we know, is your Chihuahua's best friend, next to you. It will pay to be choosy about your veterinarian. Talk to dog-owning friends whom

Grooming for good health makes good sense. Both the Long and Smooth Chihuahua's coat will benefit from regular brushing to keep it looking glossy and clean. Brushing stimulates the natural oils in the coat and also removes dead haircoat. Chihuahuas shed seasonally, which means in the Long Coat the undercoat (the soft downy white fur) is pushed out by the incoming new coat. A medium-strength bristle brush is all that is required to groom to help the undercoat along. Some Smooths have a bit of undercoat and they too will benefit from brushing during shedding season. Given the Chihuahua's tiny size, grooming can never be much of a chore.

ANAL SACS

Anal sacs, sometimes called anal glands, are located in the musculature of the anal ring, one on either side. Each empties into the rectum via a small duct. Occasionally their secretion becomes thickened and accumulates so you can readily feel these structures from the outside. If your Chihuahua is scooting across the floor dragging his rear quarters, or licking his rear, his anal sacs may need to be expressed. Placing pressure in and up towards the anus, while holding the tail, is the general routine.

The Chihuahua is one of the longest-lived dog breeds. Very few health problems exist in the breed, and it is not uncommon to see a Chihuahua live into its late teens.

MAJOR HEALTH ISSUES

Of all purebred dogs, perhaps the Chihuahua is the longest lived, most easily living into their teens—it's not uncommon to see an old-timer of 20 gracing a loving owner's home. Although health problems are minimal compared to other breeds of dogs, Chihuahuas suffer from certain heart-valve problems as well as cleft palates, hydrocephalus, cryptorchidism (retained or missing testicle), and kidney stones. Many small breeds suffer from some form of chronic heart-valve disease, and a genetic predisposition is suspected. The Chihuahua most often experiences mitral insufficiency, which is a problem with the mitral valve that separates the flow of blood on the left side of the heart.

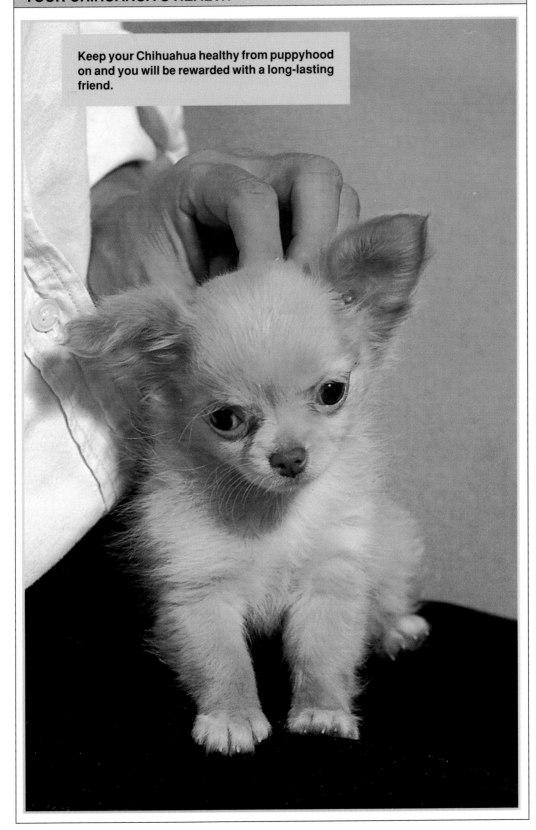

Keep your Chihuahua healthy from puppyhood on and you will be rewarded with a long-lasting friend.

In such animals, the heart is not pumping as efficiently as it should. Mild forms of mitral insufficiency can be detected in the form of heart murmurs in the aging dog; in more severe cases, a form of congestive heart failure could affect the dog. Veterinarians can detect a heart murmur early enough on and certain medications can be prescribed to help manage the condition.

Hypoglycemia, a condition marked by low blood sugar, affects many of the breeds and is reported in the Chihuahua. Signs include dizziness, general weakness, confusion and minor convulsions. Rubbing a teaspoon of sugar or corn syrup on the dog's gums is all that is needed to revive him. Don't choke him by making him swallow it—it merely needs to contact his gums. Such dogs will need to be placed on a specific diet which your veterinarian can prescribe.

Fortunately all of these conditions are limited in occurrence, and none threaten the overall likelihood that your Chihuahua will be a healthy, long-lived companion animal. Proper care and education can only help owners promote the health and longevity of their dogs.

Some tasty treats can be unhealthy for your Chihuahua. Be sure that the treats you give your pet are healthy and nutritious.

VACCINATIONS

For the continued health of your dog, owners must attend to vaccinations regularly. Your veterinarian can recommend a vaccination schedule appropriate for your dog, taking into consideration the factors of climate and geography. The basic vaccinations to protect your dog are: parvovirus, distemper, hepatitis, leptospirosis, adenovirus, parainfluenza, coronavirus, bordetella, tracheobronchitis (kennel cough), Lyme disease and rabies.

Parvovirus is a highly contagious, dog-specific disease, first recognized in 1978. Targeting the small intestine, parvo affects the stomach, and diarrhea and vomiting (with blood) are clinical signs. Although the dog can pass the infection to other dogs within three days of infection, the initial signs, which include lethargy and depression, don't display themselves until four to seven days. When affecting puppies under four weeks of age, the heart muscle is frequently attacked.

or dogs with weak immune systems can develop encephalomyelitis (brain disease) from the distemper infection. Such dogs experience seizures, general weakness and rigidity, as well as "hardpad." Since

There are a number of diseases that can be acquired and passed from one puppy to another. Make sure your Chihuahua puppy has been given all the necessary shots and that you stick to his vaccination schedule.

When the heart is affected, the puppies exhibit difficulty in breathing and experience crying and foaming at the nose and mouth.

Distemper, related to human measles, is an airborne virus that spreads in the blood and ultimately in the nervous system and epithelial tissues. Young dogs

distemper is largely incurable, prevention through vaccination is vitally important. Puppies should be vaccinated at six to eight weeks of age, with boosters at ten to 12 weeks. Older puppies (16 weeks and older) who are unvaccinated should receive no fewer than two vaccinations at three- to four-week intervals.

Hepatitis mainly affects the liver and is caused by canine adenovirus type I. Highly infectious, hepatitis often affects dogs nine to 12 months of age. Initially the virus localizes in the dog's tonsils and then disperses to the liver, kidney and eyes. Generally speaking the dog's immune system is capable of combating this virus. Canine infectious hepatitis affects dogs whose systems cannot fight off the adenovirus. Affected dogs have fever, abdominal pains, bruising on mucous membranes and gums, and experience coma and convulsions. Prevention of hepatitis exists only through vaccination at eight to ten weeks of age and then boosters three or four weeks later, then annually.

Very young puppies are particularly susceptible to canine viruses and other diseases. Talk to your breeder concerning vaccinations and other preventative medicine.

Leptospirosis is a bacterium-related disease, often spread by rodents. The organisms that spread leptospirosis enter through the mucous membranes and spread to the internal organs via the bloodstream. It can be passed through the dog's urine. Leptospirosis does not affect young dogs as consistently as the other viruses; it is reportedly regional in distribution and somewhat dependent on the immunostatus of the dog. Fever, inappetence, vomiting, dehydration, hemorrhage, kidney and eye disease can result in moderate cases.

Bordetella, called canine cough, causes a persistent hacking cough in dogs and is very contagious. Bordetella involves a virus and a bacteria: parainfluenza is the most common virus implicated; Bordetella bronchiseptica, the bacterium. Bronchitis and pneumonia result in less than 20 percent of the cases, and most dogs recover from the condition within a week to four weeks. Non-prescription medicines can help relieve the hacking cough, though nothing can cure the condition before it's run its course. Vaccination cannot guarantee protection from canine cough, but it does ward off the most common virus responsible for the condition.

Lyme disease (also called borreliosis), although known for decades, was only first diagnosed in dogs in 1984. Lyme disease can affect cats, cattle, and horses, but especially people. In the U.S., the disease is transmitted by two ticks carrying the *Borrelia burgdorferi* organism: the deer tick (*Ixodes scapularis*) and the western black-legged tick (*Ixodes pacificus*), the latter primarily affects reptiles. In Europe, *Ixodes ricinus* is responsible for spreading Lyme. The disease causes lameness, fever, joint swelling, inappetence, and lethargy. Removal of ticks from

Puppies need to receive different types of vaccination as they grow older. Consult your veterinarian and breeder for your Chihuahua's vaccination schedule.

the dog's coat can help reduce the chances of Lyme, though not as much as avoiding heavily wooded areas where the dog is most likely to contract ticks. A vaccination is

Newborn pups should remain with their mother and littermates for at least eight to ten weeks after birth. Due to the breed's diminutive size, breeders rarely let puppies go to their homes before this time.

available, though it has not been proven to protect dogs from all strains of the organism that cause the disease.

Rabies is passed to dogs and people through wildlife: in North America, principally through the skunk, fox and raccoon; the bat is not the culprit it was once thought to be. Likewise, the common image of the rabid dog foaming at the mouth with every hair on end is unlikely the truest scenario. A rabid dog exhibits difficulty eating, salivates much and has spells of paralysis and

too dangerous to manage and are commonly euthanized. Puppies are generally vaccinated at 12 weeks of age, and then annually. Although rabies is on the decline in the world community, tens of thousands of humans die each year from rabies-related incidents.

COPING WITH PARASITES

Parasites have clung to our pets for centuries. Despite our modern efforts, fleas still pester our pet's existence, and our own. All dogs itch, and fleas can make even the happiest dog a miserable, scabby

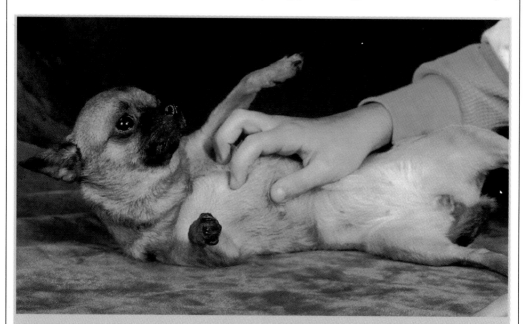

After an outdoor excursion, run your fingers through your Chihuahua's coat and inspect for parasites. All fleas and ticks should be removed from your pet's skin immediately.

awkwardness. Before a dog reaches this final state, it may experience anxiety, personality changes, irritability and more aggressiveness than is usual. Vaccinations are strongly recommended as rabid dogs are

mess. The loss of hair and habitual biting and chewing at themselves rank among the annoyances; the nuisances include the passing of tapeworms and the whole family's itching through the summer months. A

The best prevention against Lyme disease is to avoid heavily wooded areas and to thoroughly check your Chihuahua's coat for tick infestation.

full range of flea-control and elimination products are available at pet shops, and your veterinarian surely has recommendations. Sprays, powders, collars and dips fight fleas from the outside; drops and pills fight the good fight from inside. Discuss the possibilities with your vet. Not all products can be used in conjunction with one another, and some dogs may be more sensitive to certain applications than others. The dog's living quarters must be debugged as well as the dog itself. Heavy infestation may require multiple treatments.

Always check your dog for ticks carefully. Although fleas can be acquired almost anywhere, ticks are more likely to be picked up in heavily treed areas, pastures or other outside grounds (such as dog shows or obedience or field trials). Athletic, active, and hunting dogs are the most likely subjects, though any passing dog can be the host. Remember Lyme disease is passed by tick infestation.

As for internal parasites, worms are potentially dangerous for dogs and people. Roundworms, hookworms, whipworms, tapeworms, and heartworms comprise the blightsome party of troublemakers. Deworming puppies begins at around two to three weeks and continues until three months of age. Proper hygienic care of the environment is also important to prevent contamination with roundworm and hookworm eggs. Heartworm preventatives are recommended by most veterinarians, although there are some drawbacks to the regular introduction of poisons into our dogs' systems. These daily or monthly preparations also help regulate most other worms as well. Discuss worming procedures with your veterinarian.

Roundworms pose a great threat to dogs and people. They are found in the intestines of dogs, and can be passed to people through ingestion of feces-contaminated dirt. Roundworm infection can be prevented by not walking dogs in heavy-traffic people areas, by burning feces, and by curbing dogs in a responsible manner. (Of course, in most areas of the country, curbing dogs is the law.) Roundworms are typically passed from the bitch to the litter, and the bitch should be treated along with the puppies, even if she tested negative prior to whelping. Generally puppies are treated every two weeks until two months of age.

Hookworms, like roundworms, are also a danger to dogs and people. The hookworm parasite (known as *Ancylostoma caninum*) causes cutaneous larva migrans in people. The eggs of hookworms are passed in feces and become infective in shady, sandy areas. The larvae penetrate the skin of the dog, and the dog subsequently becomes infected. When swallowed, these parasites affect the intestines, lungs, windpipe, and the whole digestive system. Infected dogs suffer from anemia and lose large amounts of blood in the places where the worms latch onto the dog's intestines, etc.

Although infrequently passed to humans, whipworms are cited as one of the most common parasites in America. These elongated worms affect the intestines of the dog, where they latch on, and cause colic upset or diarrhea. Unless identified in stools passed, whipworms are difficult to diagnose. Adult worms can be

acquire tapeworms in the same way, though we are less likely to swallow fleas than dogs are. Recent studies have shown that certain rodents and wild animals have been infected with tapeworms, and dogs can be affected by catching

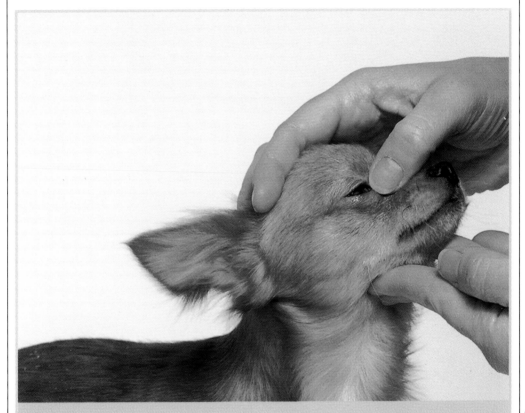

One tip for maintaining the health of your Chihuahua is to thoroughly examine his ears, eyes, mouth, nose, and coat during a grooming session. If any abnormality is apparent, consult your veterinarian immediately.

eliminated more consistently than the larvae, since whipworms exhibit unusual life cycles. Proper hygienic care of outdoor grounds is critical to the avoidance of these harmful parasites.

Tapeworms are carried by fleas, and enter the dog when the dog swallows the flea. Humans can

and/or eating these other animals. Of course, outdoor hunting dogs and terriers are more likely to be infected in this way than are your typical house dog or non-motivated hound. Treatment for tapeworm has proven very effective, and infected dogs do not show great discomfort or symptoms. When people are infected, however, the liver can be seriously damaged. Proper cleanliness is the best bet against tapeworms.

Heartworm disease is transmitted by mosquitoes and badly affects the lungs, heart and blood vessels of dogs. The larvae of *Dirofilaria immitis* enter the dog's bloodstream when bitten by an infected mosquito. The larvae take about six months to mature. Infected dogs suffer from weight loss, appetite loss, chronic coughing and general fatigue. Not all affected dogs show signs of

Just Say "Good Dog" is a new approach in teaching dogs to be good family house dogs. This manual addresses all the basic commands and responsibilities of dog ownership. Living with a dog should be a rewarding experience, and this book will show you how.

The undisputed champion of dog health books is Dr. Lowell Ackerman's encyclopedic work *Owner's Guide to Dog Health*. It covers every subject that any dog owner might need.

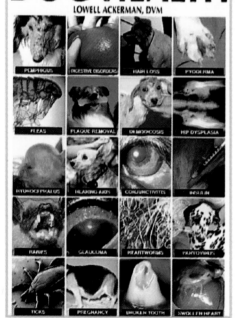

illness right away, and carrier dogs may be affected for years before clinical signs appear. Treatment of heartworm disease has been effective but can be dangerous also. Prevention as always is the desirable alternative. Ivermectin is the active ingredient in most heartworm preventatives and has proven to be successful. Check with your veterinarian for the preparation best for your dog. Dogs generally begin taking the preventatives at eight months of age and continue to do so throughout the non-winter months.